TOTALLY ROARsome DINOSAUR JOKES

This joke book is for kids looking for a totally ROARsome time.

So sit back, and get ready to roll about laughing at some of the best dinosaur jokes this side of the ice age!

No parents allowed!

Where did the Velociraptor buy its clothes?

At the dino-store!

What did the teacher say to the dinosaur that took the school bus?

"Hey! Bring that back!"

What do you call a dinosaur that keeps you awake at night?

A Bronto-snore-us!

What do pterodactyls do for fun?

Peck-nics

What do you call a dinosaur that is great at football?

A tyranno-score-us!

How do you get a dinosaur into a café?

Tea, Rex?

What do you call a one-legged dinosaur?

Eileen!

How do you know there's a dinosaur in your closet?

The door won't shut!

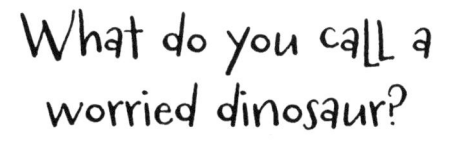

What do you call a worried dinosaur?

A nervous Rex!

What do you call a dinosaur that doesn't take a bath?

A Stink-o-saurus!

What was the most nimble dinosaur?

Tyrannosaurus Flex.

What would you get if you crossed a dinosaur with a pig?

Jurassic pork!

OINK!

What did the dinosaur use to cut wood?

A dino-saw.

Knock, knock?
Who's there?
Dinosaur.
Dinosaur who?
Dinosaurs don't go who, they go ROAAAARRRR!

Have you heard the joke about the brontosaurus' neck?

It was a really long one!

Why are dinosaur museums so secretive?

Because they have skeletons in their closets!

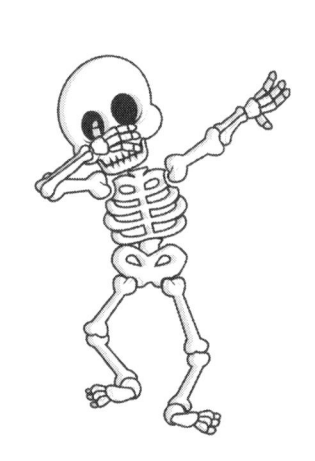

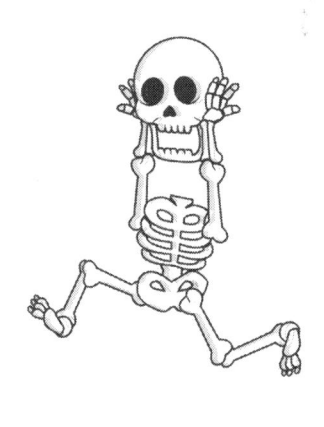

What minor injury did dinosaurs never have?

A saur thumb!

Why didn't dinosaurs tell knock-knock jokes?

Because the door hadn't been invented yet!

Knock knock!
Who's there?
Try Terry
Try Terry who?
Try Terry Tops! (Triceratops)

Why can woolly mammoths do lots of things at once?

Because they're great at multi-TUSKing

What did cavemen eat on camping trips?

Dino-smores!

Which movie do dinosaurs dislike?

Ice Age!

What do you call a limping dinosaur?

His-ankle-is-sore-us

What do you call a dinosaur who doesn't like to do anything?

A dino-bore!

What dinosaur do cowboys ride?

A bronco-saurus!

Why did the dinosaur paint her toenails red?

So that she could hide in the strawberry patch!

Why didn't the woolly mammoth jump off the iceberg?

Because it got cold feet!

Do palaeontologists like their work?

They DIG it!

Why do dinosaur parties always go wrong?

Because T-rex everything!

Knock knock!
Who's there?
Meteor.
Meteor who?

Meteor (meatier) foods taste better to me!

What would you do if a T-rex sat in front of you at the cinema?

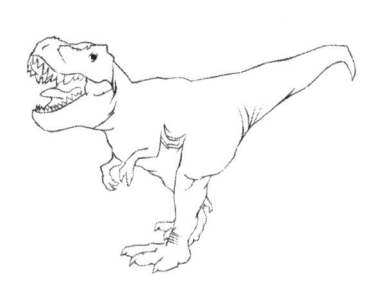

Miss most of the film!

What dinosaur can jump
higher than a house?

ALL of them.
A house can't jump!

What do you call a dinosaur
who has left its metal armour
out in the rain?

A Stegosau-rust!

What did one dinosaur egg say to another?

"Time to get cracking!"

What does a dinosaur use to play games?

A reX-box!

What does a reptile eat with its burger?

French flies!

Knock, knock?
Who's there?
Ida.
Ida who?
Ida run faster if a dinosaur was chasing me!!

What is a brontosaurus' favourite sport?

SQUASH!

What do you call a lizard that repeats itself?

A Gecho

What do you get if you cross
a dinosaur and a dog?

Jurassic bark!

What do you call
an ugly dinosaur?

An eye-saur!

What do you get if you cross a woolly mammoth and a kangaroo?

Holes all over the ice!

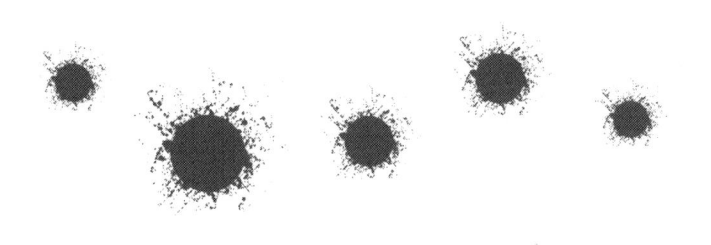

What pre-his-toric animal loves lamps?

Mam-moths

What do you call a dino that hates losing?

A 'saur loser!

Why did the brontosaurus have such a long neck?

Because its feet smelt!!

What did cavemen do to have fun?

Go clubbing!

Why don't more people look for dinosaur fossils?

Because it's beneath them!

What did the caveman think when the dinosaur found his cave?

Time to find a new cave!

Knock knock!
Who's there?
Interrupting dinosaur.
Interrupting dinosaur wh-?

ROAAAAARRR!!

How did the t-rex like its steak?

Medium-Rawr!!

What do pterodactyls do for fun?

Peck-nics!
(peck necks)

Why did the dinosaur have to be careful around its eggs?

Because they cracked under pressure!

What did a chameleon say to her kid on the first day of school?

"Don't worry, you'll blend right in!"

What was the name of the dodo's shy cousin?

The don't-don't!

Knock knock!
Who's there?
Lena.
Lena who?

Lena little too close to me I'll eat you!

What do you call a baby dinoasaur?

A Wee-rex!

Why shouldn't you ask a dinosaur to tell you a bedtime story?

Because their tales are so long!

Why can't dinosaurs use a computer?

Because they'll eat the mouse!

What did the dinosaur use to blow up a pile of rubble?

DINOmite!

What do you call a dinosaur that never gives up?

A try-try-and-try-ceraptops!

What do you call a frightened dinosaur?

A scaredactyl

What has 3 horns and 2 wheels?

A triceratops on a bike!

Knock, knock?
Who's there?
Terry.
Terry who?

It's me! Terry Dactyl!
(Pterodactyl)

What was the name of the dodo's smelly cousin?

The doo doo!

What is in the middle of dinosaurs?

S!

Why didn't the dinosaur go into the ocean?

There was something fishy about it!

Why do dinosaurs eat raw meat?

Because they don't know how to cook!

What makes more noise than one dinosaur?

TWO DINOSAURS!

ROAR

Knock knock!
Who's there?
Hide.
Hide who?
No, quickly, hide! A T-rex is coming!!

What do you call a greedy dinosaur who doesn't eat meat?

An om-nom-nom-nom-ivore

Where do dinosaurs go to buy birthday gifts?

Toy-Sau-Rus!

Why did the dinosaur cross the road?

Because chickens didn't exist back then!

Why didn't the woolly mammoth jump off the iceberg?

Because it got cold feet!

What do you call a dinosaur who needs glasses?

A do-you-think-he-saurus!

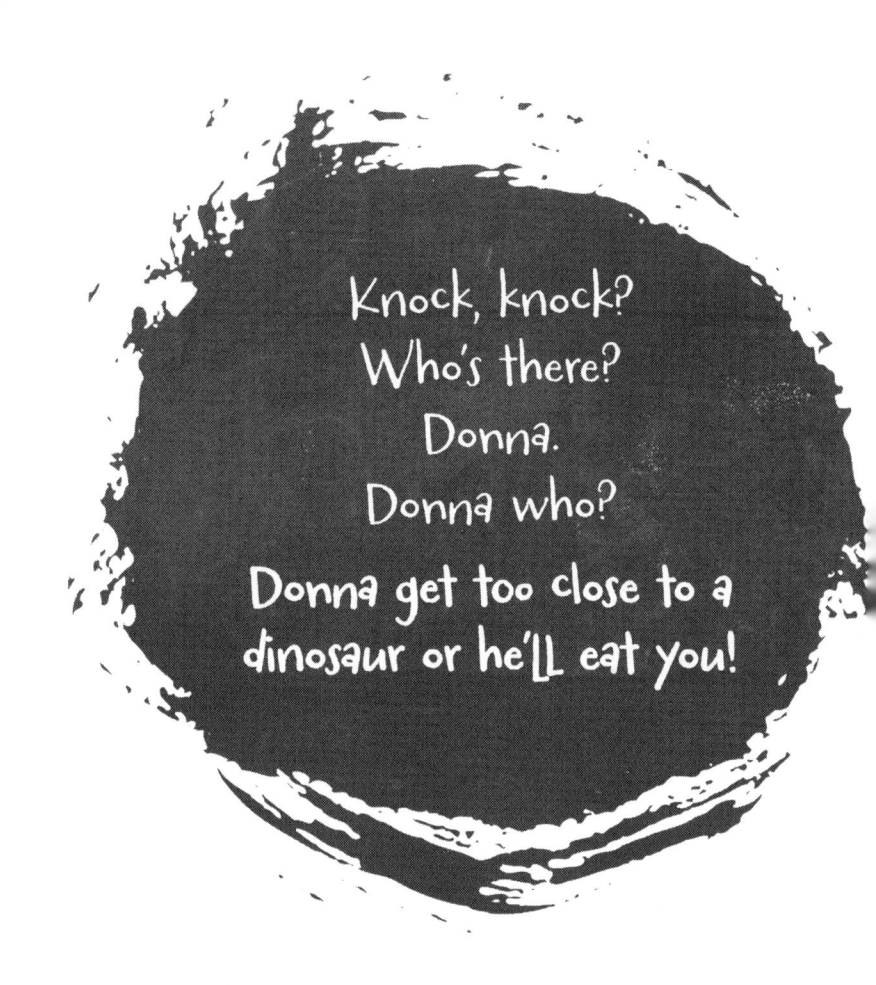

Knock, knock?
Who's there?
Donna.
Donna who?
Donna get too close to a dinosaur or he'll eat you!

What newspaper do dinosaurs read?

The Prehistoric Times.

What sound does a pterodactyl's phone make?

WING-WING!

What do you call a dinosaur who has just ran a marathon?

The I'm-mega-saurus

What should you do when a dinosaur sneezes?

Move out of the way!

What's the best way to talk to a T-Rex?

From VERY far away!

hi!

What did the dinosaurs use to drive their cars?

Fossil fuel!

Knock knock!
Who's there?
Waddle.
Waddle who?

Waddle I do with this fossil I found?

What is a reptile's favorite film?

The Lizard of Oz!!

What does the saber-tooth squirrel watch on TV?

Nut-flix!

What do you call a dinosaur that is a noisy sleeper?

Tyranno-SNOREus!

What do dinosaurs put on the kitchen floor?

Rep-tiles!

Which dinosaur had the worst eyesight?

Tyrannosaurus-SPECS!

What did the weary meteor say to the dinosaur?

Mind if I crash here?

Knock knock!
Who's there?
Willette B. Long
Willette B. Long who?
Willette B. Long before the dinosaurs find me!?

How did the chilly dinosaur connect to its computer?

Blue-tooth?

What did the dinosaur say to his girlfriend?

"You look ROAARRRsome!"

What do you call a dinosaur who knows a lot of words?

A theSAURUS

RAWR!

What do you call a group of singing dinosaurs??

A tyranno-chorus!

What do you call a dinosaur
that asks a lot of deep questions?

A philosiraptor

What do you call
a dinosaur breaking
wind?

A blast from the
past!

Why could the dinosaur not make
a decision?

His mammoth friend was a
little woolly.

Knock, knock?
Who's there?
Haven.
Haven who?
Haven you heard enough dinosaur jokes by now!?

What do you get when you cross a dinosaur with a glove?

I don't know, but don't put your hand in it!

What happened to the dinosaur who went to the gym?

He got tyran-nosaurus-pecks!

What do you get if you cross a cow with a stampeding dinosaur?

Milkshake!

MOOO

What do you get when a dinosaur jumps on your bed?

A NEW BED!

How many dinosaurs can fit in an empty box?

One! Because then it's full!

DINO DEAN

TOTALLY ROARSOME DINOSAUR JOKES

We hope that you had a ton of laughs, and that you are armed to the TOOTH to take these jokes to your friends and family!

Byeeeee!

42

Manufactured by Amazon.ca
Bolton, ON